HEAVEN'S DOOR

HEAVEN'S DOOR

ENCOUNTERING
GOD
THROUGH
SANCTIFIED
IMAGINATION

ROBERT NORRISS

Heaven's Door
Published by Robert Norriss
New Zealand

© 2019 Robert Norriss

ISBN 978-0-473-47892-6 (Softcover)
ISBN 978-0-473-47893-3 (ePUB)
ISBN 978-0-473-47894-0 (Kindle)

Editing:
Sue Beguely

Production & Typesetting:
Andrew Killick
Castle Publishing Services
www.castlepublishing.co.nz

Cover design:
Paul Smith

All Scripture quotations,
unless otherwise indicated, are taken from
the Holy Bible, New International Version®, NIV®.
Copyright ©1973, 1978, 1984, 2011 by Biblica, Inc.™
Used by permission of Zondervan.
All rights reserved worldwide.

ALL RIGHTS RESERVED

No part of this publication may be reproduced,
stored in a retrieval system, or transmitted
in any form or by any means, electronic, mechanical,
photocopying, recording or otherwise,
without prior written permission from the author.

*Since you have been raised to new life with Christ,
set your sights on the realities of heaven,
where Christ sits in the place of honour at God's right hand.
Think about the things of heaven,
not the things of earth.
(Colossians 3:1–2, NLT)*

FOREWORD

I have been friends with Robert for over 21 years. Over that time, I have had the pleasure to observe, first-hand, the journey of discovery that has led to this book.

It has been my joy to see Robert develop the intimacy with God he writes about in these pages.

Personality-wise, Robert sits strongly at the cognitive, logical and reasoning end of the spectrum, but his passion to *experience* God – not just know about him intellectually – has led him to push his own inner boundaries and develop the ability to hear God's voice consistently.

As a pastor, I have noticed that many Christians struggle to hear from God. They have very few 'God spoke to me' moments. Most of us crave God's touch on our being, but, for whatever reason, we can find it hard to experience that contact.

Robert has found a way past these blockages, through the use of what he terms 'sanctified imagination'.

His great desire is to share what he has learnt so that others can have a deeper relationship with God.

Robert's journey has been real and life-changing. He's still as intelligent and logical as he always was, but now a whole new ability has arisen in his life – the ability Jesus spoke about for all his followers – that we would hear his voice, experience him and see his kingdom come.

I encourage you to read this book and experiment with the exercises each chapter contains. Your walk with Jesus will never be the same.

John Alpe
Senior Pastor
St Albans Baptist Church, Christchurch

CONTENTS

Acknowledgements	11
Introduction	13
Connections	17
The Beginning	21
Exercise 1: A Favourite Place	27
Why?	29
Exercise 2: Rest and Relax	33
Equipped	35
Exercise 3: The Throne Room	41
Designed	43
Exercise 4: Thankful to God	49
Positioned	51
Exercise 5: Bringing the Word to Life	55
Activate	57
Exercise 6: Yes, Lord	65
Practise	69
Exercise 7: Keep It Simple	75
Grow	77
About the Author	81

ACKNOWLEDGEMENTS

There is an endless list of people who have helped me on my life journey for whom I am so appreciative. However, there are some special people I want to thank without whose help this book would never have been written. Firstly, my wife Denise for her inspiration; my pastors, John and Sandra Alpe, for their help, guidance and encouragement; Anna Button and Gill North for their editing and help in structuring the text and, finally, John Massam for his support and advice.

INTRODUCTION

Most Christians I meet would like to hear God speak to them more. I have discovered this is not only possible, it is vital to becoming the people God planned us to be.

It took a lot of work to understand my identity as a cherished and equipped son of God, and the work is ongoing. Outwardly I may have appeared to be a confident, assured person, but inwardly I experienced conflict, doubt and insecurity.

I have been an elder at St Albans Baptist church in Christchurch for nearly 20 years. The very day after I was appointed as an elder, the senior pastor, John Alpe, called my work office to get my opinion on an issue. When my secretary told me that John Alpe was on the phone, my very first thought was, 'Oh no! What have I done wrong already?'

Similarly, around 2008, I was invited by John to attend a retreat in Hanmer designed for Baptist church leaders to restore spiritual health and to seek God. This was the second time the event had been run and around 30 to 40 leaders attended. As I looked through the names of the other people who would be attending, I thought to myself, 'What right do I have to be there among these amazing people?'

These two situations, and my default reactions, revealed a lot about the state of my identity. I felt inadequate and insignificant and I believe that similar default reactions hold many Christians back from stepping into all God has planned for them. We hold back from running into the opportunities he presents in all areas of our lives because we do not realise the authority and significance God has bestowed on us. Yet his desire is to make us more than adequate and he calls us to be significant.

Can you imagine what would happen if all God's followers woke up tomorrow and lived out the day in full awareness of who Christ has called them to be? How many conversations about God and what he has done would occur in our workplaces, families and networks as we boldly brought him up and made the most of the opportunities God creates every day? How many new, powerful, life-changing ministries would be started as people's fear and shame were removed and followers armed themselves to pursue the ideas God has given them?

We were made in God's likeness and consequently we have his attributes and his authority to advance his kingdom here on earth. It's what we are made for! The very first chapter of the Bible describes how we are created in his image, how he blessed us and gave us authority. Our identity and who we are called to be was the first thing God described in his Word to us.

It is no coincidence then that Eve's identity was the very thing that Satan used to convince her to succumb to temptation. He told her, 'You will be like God,' when she already was!

Satan continues to attack our identity today. The Devil

knows that Christians who fully realise who they are and the power and authority they have as sons or daughters of God, are people who endanger his mission. He understands how much God's kingdom would advance if all Christians realised their potential and he uses every means possible to stop that advance.

One of the Devil's key strategies to stop us realising our potential and living in our full identity is to attack our prayer life. If we are not talking and spending quality time with God, how can we hear him speak lovingly to us and hear his thoughts on who we are and where he wants us to go? To grow fully into our identity we need to hear God speak regularly and frequently.

> Do you not know?
> Have you not heard?
> The LORD is the everlasting God,
> the Creator of the ends of the earth.
> He will not grow tired or weary,
> and his understanding no one can fathom.
> He gives strength to the weary
> and increases the power of the weak.
> Even youths grow tired and weary,
> and young men stumble and fall;
> but those who hope in the LORD
> will renew their strength.
> They will soar on wings like eagles;
> they will run and not grow weary,
> they will walk and not be faint.
> (Isaiah 40:28–31)

In Isaiah 40 the prophet beautifully tells us that as we 'hope in the Lord' – as we wait on God and receive input from him – we will receive all we need to live out the plan and purpose God has for us. Hearing God speak is essential for realising our identity and having strength for the journey. This book has been written to help you become the person God designed you to be.

We do not grow in our identity or become more effective by increasing how much we say to God. Jesus said:

> And when you pray, do not keep on babbling like pagans, for they think they will be heard because of their many words. Do not be like them, for your Father knows what you need before you ask him. (Matthew 6:7–8)

We grow by listening to God and having better conversations with him.

My hope is that as you read the following pages, you will discover a tool which will result in you having deep and meaningful conversations with our Almighty God, and realising your identity as his child more and more. Using this tool and having God speak to me regularly has transformed my life. I pray the same for you.

CONNECTIONS

'In the last days,' God says,
'I will pour out my Spirit on all people.
Your sons and daughters will prophesy,
your young men will see visions,
your old men will dream dreams.' (Acts 2:17)

As the owner of an engineering maintenance company, I have a lot to do with machinery. Machines, like humans, have good days and bad. Some days they have problems and other days things go well and they fulfil the purpose for which they were designed. However, no matter what type of day it is, machines will never have imagination. A machine doesn't daydream or decide to do an activity outside of its design parameters. Machines lack free will, or the capacity for free thought. People, on the other hand, have been given free will, and one of the facets of free will is imagination. Imagination is essential in terms of thinking of doing things correctly or doing things wrongly.

We often use our imagination in negative ways. We imagine disasters happening and consequently worry. We imagine something inappropriate and struggle to keep our minds pure. I believe that for many years the church has focused more on the cognitive part of the brain and shied away from the imaginative part of the brain, to our loss.

When Jesus redeemed us, his redemption included our imagination. Surrendered and submitted to Jesus, our imagination is sanctified and becomes a powerful tool for connecting to the spirit realm. It allows the Holy Spirit to reveal powerful truth at a heart level instead of just a head level.

When the apostle Peter quoted the prophet Joel as above, he included you and me in the designation of *all people*. Peter said the Holy Spirit would be poured out on us. Through this baptism, we can prophesy, see visions, and dream. Prophecy, visions and dreams flow from the imaginative part of our brain. They come from the Spirit and flow out through our imagination.

Seeing is so important for God's kingdom to advance. Why would a Christian dedicate their life to working in a poverty-stricken area, if they couldn't see the possibility of a better future for the people? Why would we stop and minister to a sick person if we couldn't see the possibility of their healing or comfort? Why help, minister, encourage or bless people at all if we can't see the gold within them?

The more I have activated my imagination, the more I have been able to see and *take thoughts from heaven* and through this, release God's kingdom on earth. Why is that? Because God's kingdom grows through faith and faith is a seeing force. For faith to be activated, we must be able to see a possibility that doesn't yet exist, and to see that possibility requires our imagination. Faith comes from hearing God's word and is outworked through seeing a different future to that which presently exists.

Most of my Christian life has been based mainly in a cognitive framework. Even on the day of my salvation at the age of 13, I made a logical decision. I realised that if God was real, the only logical choice was to follow him, and if he wasn't real, it didn't matter. Based on that logic, I chose to surrender to Jesus. In my faith experience, imagination has been largely dormant and unexercised. In recent years I have been learning to grow and develop my spiritual imagination. It has been a discovery process that has been a blessing not only to me, but also to the many people I have ministered to.

Sanctified imagination is a term I have coined for exercises that strengthen our imagination 'muscle', increase our encounters with God and deepen our understanding of who we are and who God is. Sanctified imagination encompasses the thoughts God puts in our minds as we commune with him. In the following chapters you will read about aspects of my experience and what I have learnt.

As you read this book I hope that I can:

- help you to understand that you are designed for God-encounters
- provide some insight and tools to help you grow in the experience of encountering God in your prayer life, especially through your imagination
- help you to hear God's voice better.

At the end of each chapter there are exercises to help you experience and hear God with your imagination. But first let me take you to the beginning...

THE BEGINNING

Sanctified imagination connects us with the Father, Son and Holy Spirit, unlocking pathways that were always destined for believers to use.

I had always struggled to feel a connection with God or to experience manifestations of the Holy Spirit. To me, it seemed like there were two camps. The first camp consisted of people who didn't seem to have any trouble 'falling down' when being ministered to or having fits of laughter as they were impacted by the joy of the Spirit. The second camp was made up of people like me who, despite having deep faith and belief in Jesus, don't seem to feel anything when ministered to. I would have people who were full of faith lay hands on me for a fresh filling of the Holy Spirit and, as much as I would hope to experience a manifestation of the Spirit, there appeared to be nothing. I say 'appeared' because I believe that when we ask, God always does something, even if we don't see the evidence immediately.

I knew I was a follower of Jesus, filled with the Holy Spirit, and had a deep faith in Jesus. During my years of being a Christian, I have experienced miracles and healings, both personally and as I have prayed for others. While ministering to people, God has worked through me with words of knowledge and prophetic messages, as well as allowing manifestations of the Spirit to take place in the people receiving ministry.

On many occasions Jesus has spoken to me out of the Bible. For example, God spoke to me through the Bible when I was considering marriage. I have been married to my best friend, Denise, for over 30 years. When we were dating, our biggest desire, concern and hope was to know that God wanted us to be married and that we were in his will.

Soon after we recognised that we would like to be married, Denise came over to visit. She said she had been praying and that God had given her a verse from the Bible she believed was meant for us. She further believed that if we were in God's will, then God would give me the same verse. This became our test, rather like Gideon putting out a fleece to be sure God was with him.

For me to receive the same verse as Denise meant God would have to reveal it. After some fervent prayer, I felt God had given me a verse which I shared with Denise and, praise God, it was the same verse God had given her. I think it is important to note that my sensing this was the right verse didn't come with any amazing signs or by hearing an audible voice. It just came through a quiet assurance.

There was a further confirmation on our wedding day: without our discussing with anyone else that God had revealed this verse to us, on our wedding day the pastor preached from the same passage. God is amazing.

Yet despite many similar occurrences when I received nudges from God through quiet assurance, I still couldn't say that I felt God, and rarely experienced manifestations

The Beginning

of the Spirit, at least not like those I had observed in other people.

As a result of years of not experiencing God in the way other people seemed to experience him, I had begun to believe that God just wanted me to live by faith and that he hadn't wired me to have encounters with him. This was a lie, of course, but at the time it convinced me that having God-encounters didn't really matter.

Once I had started to believe this lie, I found myself consoling others with these thoughts when they weren't experiencing God either. This lie was rooted in my belief system for nearly 30 years.

However, in recent times, God has led me to discover sanctified imagination and this journey has shown me how wrong I was. I no longer believe the lie that not encountering God is part of how God designed me. I have replaced this lie with the truth that we are each designed and destined to encounter God. It is our birthright.

Put simply, sanctified imagination makes use of our God-given creativity. We are made in God's image and God is creative. Sanctified imagination uses our imagination to experience Jesus and talk openly with him.

The first time I discovered what God can do with our imagination occurred long before I started calling this process sanctified imagination. I was ministering to a person at a Christian gathering; I encouraged them to imagine walking towards a tree that stood by a lake, to sit at the foot of the tree and imagine Jesus was sitting with them. I then asked if they could see Jesus. They said they could. I suggested they listen to what Jesus wanted to say to them. As the person did this, they revealed that they felt an incredible peace and that Jesus had spoken encouragingly to them.

Over the next few years, I repeatedly felt prompted to do something similar with people. On one occasion I was ministering to a businessman needing God's help in his business. I took him through a process of surrendering his business to Jesus. Once he had done this, I asked him to imagine himself at his boardroom table with Jesus sitting on the other side as the CEO of his business. I encouraged him to ask Jesus what he wanted to say. He started prophesying about himself and his business and had an awesome God-encounter.

Andrew is another example of someone whose journey with God has been powerfully impacted by his imagination. Andrew was very wary about using his imagination because of publications he had read which taught that meditation and imagination weren't godly. We were both attending the Baptist leaders' annual prayer and fasting time held in Hanmer and I felt prompted to go over and pray for him. This was the first time I had met him. Like me, up to this point, Andrew's God-encounters had been limited.

I asked Andrew if he liked tramping, to which he responded, 'Yes'. So, in the safe environment of the meeting, I encouraged Andrew to imagine himself walking in the bush, with Jesus walking beside him. I then encouraged Andrew to ask Jesus what he wanted to say to him. For the next half an hour Andrew was powerfully impacted as the Holy Spirit did a work in him. Andrew had a very significant God-encounter which radically changed his beliefs and thinking.

I recently caught up with Andrew and asked what had

changed for him since that time. Andrew shared how his understanding has been opened up in a positive way about the power of our imagination. Andrew now uses his imagination to bring Bible stories to life. He also finds using his imagination powerful in corporate prayer meetings as he perceives what the Spirit is doing. Andrew says he is a changed man.

As I have observed people being impacted by God through their imagination, I have had lots of questions about what was happening. Was this actually a godly thing? Was it idolatry? Could our imagination be a positive spiritual place? I spent time studying Scripture and, finally, I started trying to use my imagination in my own relationship with Jesus. The power, the transformation, the God-encounters and the revelation I have experienced since then have been remarkable.

EXERCISE 1:
A Favourite Place

When using your imagination, especially at the start, closing your eyes is helpful to reduce distractions. Having some instrumental music playing in the background can be helpful. I searched 'Soaking Instrumental' on Spotify and find it perfect.

It is important to ask Jesus to lead you, to take you through the exercise and speak to you. Submit this time to God and ensure he is in charge.

When ministering, I often find having people imagine themselves in a favourite place with Jesus works well. It could be some favourite scenery, a favourite chair, a special place. For one person I was ministering to, it was hunting. For someone else it was having coffee. For me, when I first started using my imagination, it was running along a beach with Jesus running beside me.

The beauty of a favourite place is that it is familiar and thus easier for us to imagine it. I have also found Jesus loves what we love and enjoys meeting us in our favourite places.

So why don't you pause right now, get relaxed, close your eyes, have some music quietly playing, and start to imagine yourself in your favourite place. Within your imagination

Heaven's Door

look for Jesus; imagine he is there with you. Don't worry about detail or clarity, just relax. Once you have imagined Jesus with you, ask him what he wants to say to you. You may want to write it down.

For some of you this will have been a powerful time. For others, you may have struggled. If initially it is a struggle, don't give up! As you continue through the following chapters, I hope you will discover helpful tips and develop the practice further. Isn't it great that God made us all different?

WHY?

> Do not conform to the pattern of this world, but be transformed by the renewing of your mind. Then you will be able to test and approve what God's will is – his good, pleasing and perfect will. (Romans 12:2)

During a sanctified imagination time, Jesus took me to a garden and said, 'This is the garden of your heart and mind.' Jesus then went on to explain many things and told me that when a person comes to him, their garden is a mess. It is full of weeds and has poor soil. Jesus explained that the first thing he does is plant the Tree of Life in the middle of each new garden. He then starts to clear away weeds, which can be a lengthy process as some weeds have deep roots and take a long time to be removed completely. Jesus explained that these weeds represent bad beliefs.

I observed an area of my garden that looked like the soil had been freshly worked over. I looked at Jesus and he smiled. 'That's an area of bad beliefs we have been working on lately. As we pull those out, we prepare the soil for new beliefs to grow.' In other parts of the garden there appeared to be healthy, fruitful growth. Jesus handed me a spade and invited me to start digging. I then noticed a river running beside the garden and instinctively I knew it was the River of Life. Jesus pointed to a part of the garden and said, 'That part of your heart is quite dry and needs water so we are going to dig an irrigation channel.'

God has called each of us to be people of influence, destined to transform the world. God wants us to be everything he designed us to be and to achieve his good, pleasing and perfect will.

Unfortunately, we often still have weeds planted in the garden of our hearts and minds – weeds that have been sown through our past experience. These weeds can include things that have happened or things that have been said. The weeds have deep roots and can limit our future.

We need our minds renewed with new beliefs from God's Word so that we are transformed into the person God already sees us to be. The truth is that he sees you as strong, powerful, confident and an awesome member of his family.

> Then you will know the truth, and the truth will set you free. (John 8:32)

As we allow God to speak truth into our hearts and minds, he releases us from the weeds of wrong beliefs and brings freedom to our lives. He enables us to walk in our true identity and go after our destiny.

Most of us will, at some stage, wonder if we are just treading water or if there a reason for what we are doing. Having Jesus speak to us regularly solves that problem.

> The weapons we fight with are not the weapons of the world. On the contrary, they have divine power to

demolish strongholds. We demolish arguments and every pretension that sets itself up against the knowledge of God, and we take captive every thought to make it obedient to Christ. (2 Corinthians 10:4–5)

As we are transformed, we fulfil God's good, pleasing and perfect will. Transformation comes from renewing our minds. Our minds are renewed as we demolish strongholds and bring every thought into obedience to Christ. Sanctified imagination is one tool I have found that really helps in this process.

EXERCISE 2:
Rest and Relax

> To him who is able to keep you from stumbling and to present you before his glorious presence without fault and with great joy... (Jude 1:24)

The exercises in this book are designed to help us hear Jesus speak and to enjoy God's presence. Sometimes all we need is to feel his warmth, his touch, his goodness.

For this exercise, find a relaxing spot and get comfortable. Imagine yourself walking beside the River of Life. Follow the river upstream towards the throne of God.

As you get close to the throne, notice that it is elevated and sits on rough, unfashioned rock. A waterfall flows out from the throne and feeds the River of Life. Move forward and stand under the waterfall. Imagine the water massaging your aches and pains and washing away your troubles and cares. Stay there until you feel refreshed.

Next, allow yourself to lie back in the pool at the base of the waterfall and start floating down the river. As you float down the river, you come to the Tree of Life, which I imagine to be like a canopy over the river. Notice the different colours of the leaves and imagine breathing in the freshness and newness of life.

When you have passed under the Tree of Life, allow yourself to float to the edge of the river. Climb up onto the bank and lie down, allowing the warmth and light of God to soak into your body and soul.

I hope you are now feeling rested. It is OK to fall asleep in God's presence.

I wonder if what we see in our imagination is a glimpse of what heaven looks like? However, the purpose is not to gain knowledge about what heaven is like, but to attain intimacy with God.

EQUIPPED

> My sheep listen to my voice; I know them, and they follow me. (John 10:27)

I am amazed at how little I have heard Jesus speak to me during my 40 years of being a Christian. As I have talked to many other Christians about hearing God, I find not hearing Jesus speak is a common problem, to our loss. Whenever our church ran conferences there were two workshops we could be certain would be well attended: one would be on the topic of knowing God's will, the other on hearing God speak. This experience provided additional confirmation that many Christians are not living in the power of John 10:27. They are not hearing and following.

I have been through times when my prayers were like shopping lists. I would go through the list of items I wanted to pray about – my spouse, my children, work, the church, the country – and I would ask God to help in these areas. Then I would go off and live life, not waiting for answers. Consequently, my prayer times often felt dry and I would feel guilty that I was not praying enough.

If that also describes you at present, if you identify with this, please don't feel guilty. I think we have all been there.

The good news is that we are equipped to hear God. That is if you are one of Jesus' sheep.

John 10:27 is a great verse. In this verse Jesus says his sheep listen to him. How powerful is that! The only prerequisite for hearing Jesus is to be one of his sheep. Hearing Jesus doesn't depend on going to Bible college, fasting, or living an exceptionally loving and holy life. These are all good things, but we do not need them in order to hear Jesus. We need only to be a Christ-follower, one of his sheep. Jesus is saying, if we believe in him, we are equipped to listen to him, to hear him, to encounter him.

God is incredibly creative, and there is no limit to the ways he can communicate with us. It is God's responsibility to communicate. It is our responsibility to listen.

I am now regularly hearing Jesus 'speak'. One of the ways I know it is Jesus, is that often what Jesus talks about does not appear to have been triggered by any recent experience or thought. What I mean is that usually I have not been thinking about the topic that Jesus brings to mind. Sometimes I did not even know the topic was important, and yet what Jesus said has always been something I needed to hear.

On one occasion I was in bed and I imagined myself sitting with Jesus beside the River of Life. Jesus jumped to his feet saying, 'Come on.' So, I got up and followed. We went over to a spiral staircase and climbed up. When we arrived at the top I found we were standing in a library. I don't know if there is a library in heaven, but it is certainly possible since Scripture talks about books in heaven.

I felt Jesus say to me, 'These writings are the record of what the Father speaks. The Father continually speaks because it is his Word that holds everything together. If the Father stopped speaking, existence would stop. Books are continually added because the Father continually speaks.'

As previously mentioned, I do not know where this picture of a library came from. I hadn't been to a library recently, hadn't talked about libraries or thought about libraries, and yet this was where my imagination went. This is an example of what happens through being equipped to hear God.

From the entrance of the main room we walked across to the other side and came to some corridors. Jesus started walking down one, so I followed. As we walked along the corridor, I noticed many smaller rooms off to each side. Jesus said to me, 'Each of these rooms is for a person who has lived or is still living on earth and inside each room are the records of what the Father has spoken about that person.' Instantly, we came to a room which I knew was significant for me. Jesus said, 'This is your room.' I went inside and observed shelf upon shelf full of books and was astonished by how much was written, indicating how much God had spoken about me. I also noticed there were empty shelves which I assumed were for future things God was going to say.

And then I fell asleep.

The reason I share this story is to demonstrate that not hearing God's voice or communication has nothing to do with God not speaking. God is continually speaking. If this library exists in heaven, then you too have a room full of books which are the record of everything God has spoken to you and about you. If we are not hearing God's voice, it is only because we are not listening.

And yet Jesus says we are fully equipped to hear his

voice. We are his sheep. We have the ability. Perhaps we don't know how or perhaps we need practice.

There are many things we can do to develop hearing God's voice. Sanctified imagination is a way I have found to open up a whole new dimension of communication with God.

The reason I believe this works so well is that it makes use of being designed, equipped, and positioned to encounter our Lord and Saviour, Jesus. Our imagination connects with our spirit.

We have everything we need for God-encounters. God has equipped us with all the tools required for us to experience and hear him.

There are many incredible verses in the Bible which equip us to hear God more. When we start to believe them, our minds are transformed and the way we live starts to change. We begin to hear him more and live our lives accordingly.

An example of this occurred while I was ministering recently to a church leader who was about to start a new role. The following words of Jesus came to mind:

'For my yoke is easy and my burden is light.' (Matthew 11:30)

I proceeded to prophesy over the pastor that God wanted to remind him of this verse. Jesus' promised him a light burden. Whenever he felt the burden getting heavy, then he needed to realise something was out of alignment, and he was carrying things he didn't need to carry.

Since then, I have realised this is a great verse and have

started applying it to my own belief system. If I start getting stressed or worried about life, I stop and realise that part of my life is out of alignment, that I am carrying burdens I don't need to carry. Normally it means I have stopped putting my trust in God concerning whatever is causing me worry. I now try and bring my worry to Jesus. I start listening to Jesus as I hand things back to him and do this until I reach a place of peace again. After doing this, I am only carrying the things Jesus intends me to carry because his yoke is easy, his burden is light. Life is released again. I am more equipped.

> I sought the Lord, and he answered me; he delivered me from all my fears. (Psalm 34:4)

Sanctified imagination is a great way to seek the Lord, to hear his will and receive guidance. He will answer and impart wisdom for our situations. I bring my worries to Jesus and receive peace.

Not only are we equipped to encounter God, we are also designed and positioned for such encounters, as we will discover in the next chapters.

EXERCISE 3:
The Throne Room

> Then the angel showed me the river of the water of life, as clear as crystal, flowing from the throne of God and of the Lamb down the middle of the great street of the city. On each side of the river stood the tree of life, bearing twelve crops of fruit, yielding its fruit every month. And the leaves of the tree are for the healing of the nations.
> (Revelation 22:1–2)

God's throne room is one of my favourite places to be in my imagination. I have had lots of incredible experiences there.

For this exercise, read the verses from Revelation 22 again. You may also want to read Revelation 4. Imagine yourself going over to the River of Life and drinking from its waters. These waters are a representation of the Holy Spirit and, as you imagine drinking, believe by faith that you are receiving a fresh infilling of the Spirit. Try making a drinking action as well.

After you have drunk your fill, go over to the Tree of Life. Imagine different types of fruit. The apostle Paul names some of them:

> But the fruit of the Spirit is love, joy, peace, patience,

kindness, goodness, faithfulness, gentleness and self-control. Against such things there is no law. (Galatians 5:22–23)

Choose a fruit. What name is written on it? Take, eat and then try out some action that represents the fruit you have eaten. Love might be prostrating yourself on the floor before God; peace might be slow, deep-breathing exercises; joy might be laughing. Be creative.
Take your time doing this and enjoy whatever God does for you with this exercise.

DESIGNED

> Therefore, if anyone is in Christ, that person is a new creation: The old has gone, the new has come! (2 Corinthians 5:17)

In some ways this is an unusual verse. What does it mean to be a new creation? When we were saved, did we disappear and then reappear as something completely different? When I came to faith, my body didn't suddenly disappear to be replaced by some brand new body, appealing as that prospect is. No, this verse is referring to a spiritual creation, not a physical one.

At your point of salvation, something new in the spiritual realm was created for you.

Why a new creation?
A new creation is needed if we are going to encounter God. If we were to encounter God in our current physical form, we wouldn't survive. When Moses wanted to see God, God hid Moses in some rocks so he saw only a very small part of God. Without the protection God provided for the encounter, Moses' body would have dissolved and ceased to exist.

This is why, when we read accounts of people in the Old Testament seeing angels, their experience is often mixed with fear and dread.

> And the LORD said, 'I will cause all my goodness to pass in front of you, and I will proclaim my name, the LORD, in your presence. I will have mercy on whom I will have mercy, and I will have compassion on whom I will have compassion. But,' he said, 'you cannot see my face, for no one may see me and live.'
>
> Then the LORD said, 'There is a place near me where you may stand on a rock. When my glory passes by, I will put you in a cleft in the rock and cover you with my hand until I have passed by. Then I will remove my hand and you will see my back; but my face must not be seen.' (Exodus 33:19–23)

Our old, physical self is not able to encounter God, at least not in the way we want to encounter him as followers of Jesus. God's goodness is just too pure for that. This is the reason a new creation is so important. We need to be made of better stuff. We need to be made of stuff designed for God-encounters.

Once, as a young child, I didn't think our fire was starting very well so I had a brainwave: I would put a bit of petrol on the wood to help it light. I went out to the garage and poured a small amount of petrol into a plastic container and ran back inside. As I reached the fire, the plastic dissolved in my hands and the petrol and plastic spilled onto the floor. Fortunately, the petrol didn't come into contact with the fire or that might have been the end of the house!

The plastic of the container I used wasn't designed to contain the petrol. It needed to be made of better stuff.

Similarly, when we are saved, a new creation is required to give us the capacity to encounter God.

What is the new creation?

> I tell you the truth, no one can see the kingdom of God unless they are born again. (John 3:3)

Think about this verse carefully, as it is crucial to our understanding. Jesus uses the phrase *born again* to refer specifically to our becoming part of God's kingdom. When we accept Jesus as our Saviour and Lord, we are choosing to accept God as our king and we become subjects of his kingdom.

Today we often hear or use the phrase *being born again* to refer to the fact that we have accepted Jesus as our Saviour. However, I'm not sure if we appreciate what the phrase really means.

Let us recap briefly and gather together the points we have considered so far in this chapter. Firstly, the apostle Paul says when we come to faith we are new creations. Secondly, Jesus says we need to be born again to see God's kingdom.

Isn't it interesting that the terms *being created* and *being born* are very similar in meaning. Both words imply that something new has been made, or has come into existence. We have already established that the new thing isn't physical, so what is it?

Fortunately, Jesus gave some clues about what being

born again means. Jesus talked about the birthing process as one of 'being born of water and the Spirit.'

We are born of water as we repent, turning from our old, ungodly ways and coming back to God. This is symbolised by the waters of baptism, dying to our old nature and rising again with our new nature.

Being born of the Spirit is the aspect I want to focus on. Through the salvation process, we are born of the Holy Spirit. The Holy Spirit gives birth, and during birth something new comes alive. What is birthed?

> Flesh gives birth to flesh, but the Spirit gives birth to spirit. (John 3:6)

Spirit gives birth to spirit. The Holy Spirit gives birth to our spirit, regenerating it. It is really important to understand this.

Both the new creation and the new birth are spiritual in nature. At the point of our salvation, the Holy Spirit gives birth and our spirit is born anew.

I have taken time getting to this point to make sure we understand it because it is so important with regard to our ability to encounter God. We know in nature that a cat gives birth to a cat, a dog gives birth to a dog and so on. Further, what is birthed carries the likeness and the DNA of the parent. There is a popular trend now for people to get their DNA checked so they can confirm their heritage. Why can they do this? Because what is born carries the DNA of the parents.

Similarly, when our spirit is birthed by the Holy Spirit, our spirit is of the same nature as the Holy Spirit and carries the same sort of characteristics. DNA is a physical thing, but spiritually, we have the same spiritual DNA as the Holy Spirit.

Why is this important?
This is the point. Before our salvation we did not have the capability to encounter God as saviour, friend, comforter and father because our spirit was dead to God and our physical body could not handle God-encounters. However, after experiencing salvation everything changes. We now have everything we need to encounter God. Our spirit is born, designed, ready and empowered for God-encounters. In the same way as a baby is designed to encounter its mother and father, so we are designed to encounter our spiritual parents, Father, Son and Holy Spirit, having been born of the Spirit.

This was a truth I did not understand for many years. The lie I had come to accept was that God had not designed me for encounters with him. However, as born-again Christians we are each designed for God-encounters. It is our birthright; it is what we were created for. I now know I am designed for God-encounters. It is who I am. I don't deserve it and it has nothing to do with my personality type. Purely and simply, I can have God-encounters because it is the way God made and birthed me when I became a Christian. If you are a follower of Christ, you are made for God-encounters and he is waiting to meet with you.

We are designed and equipped for meeting with and hearing God.

God is amazing, diverse and creative by nature. The encounters he has designed for you may be quite different to the encounters he has designed for me. We are all unique, incredible creations of God. We should expect a diversity of encounters. While each of our encounters will be different, the point is that we should all have them.

EXERCISE 4:
Thankful to God

Know that the Lord is God.
It is he who made us, and we are his;
we are his people, the sheep of his pasture.
Enter his gates with thanksgiving
and his courts with praise;
give thanks to him and praise his name.
(Psalm 100:3–4)

Being thankful is one of the most powerful tools we have to succeed in our Christian walk. This psalm encourages us to enter his gates with thanksgiving and see what new things he wants to reveal.

For this exercise, get yourself relaxed and start to thank God. To start with, you could thank him for who he is and what he is doing. Here are some suggestions:

- God's goodness
- Your family
- Friends
- Health
- Work
- School

- Your church
- Provision
- Guidance
- Giftings
- Support through trouble
- Trials
- His presence

You can keep going. Even if you are in a difficult situation, there will always be things you can thank God for because God is always redeeming difficult situations for good. There is always something. Thanksgiving is a key that makes room for more of God, which enables the cycle of more blessing and even more things to be thankful for.

As you are starting to be thankful, close your eyes and activate your imagination. Imagine you are standing before a gate or door. You are free to imagine what the gate or door looks like. I like to imagine a fence made with large stones and a stone archway over a wooden gate with a rolling meadow on the other side. You might like to imagine a different scene. What do your walls look like? What is on this side you are standing on, and what might be on the other side?

In your imagination, as you are being thankful, imagine the gate or door opens and that Jesus is standing on the other side. He takes you by the hand and invites you in.

What do you discover on the other side of the gate and what does Jesus say to you? You may want to write it down.

POSITIONED

But because of his great love for us, God, who is rich in mercy, made us alive with Christ even when we were dead in transgressions – it is by grace you have been saved. And God raised us up with Christ and seated us with him in the heavenly realms in Christ Jesus... (Ephesians 2:4–6)

I love the picture C.S. Lewis paints in *The Last Battle*, which is part of the Narnia series. He describes a world which reveals more and more of itself the further up and the further in you go. The further up and the further in the characters travel, the more real and vibrant Narnia becomes.

This imagery has increased my understanding of the spiritual realm. C.S. Lewis pointed out that as we focus increasingly on heaven and God's kingdom, our understanding of the heavenly realm grows. I believe the spirit world is far more real than the physical world our senses are used to.

When our time on this planet comes to an end, we will receive a new body which is more alive, more real and more solid than anything on this planet. This new body is necessary if we are to enjoy the purity, glory and splendour of heaven. However, our reborn spirit is already designed for heaven so it does not need to be changed.

Paul says that we are positioned in heaven. Not only do we exist in the natural world, we also exist in heaven, within Christ.

In Ephesians 2, Paul says that not only is Jesus seated in heavenly realms, but so are we: 'God raised us up with Christ and seated us with him in the heavenly realms in Christ Jesus.' We are here on earth and we are also in heaven. Our three-dimensional thinking makes this concept difficult to understand, but the implication is really important. Wherever we are on earth, heaven is with us.

I find it incredibly empowering to know that heaven is with us.

We are seated in heavenly realms with God, ready and positioned for encounters. Ephesians 2 is relevant *now*. It is not something that happens when our body dies, but is a reality now. We are positioned in God and thus we are able to have encounters with him.

This means that as we go about our day – whatever we do, wherever we go – not only are we positioned in that location in a physical sense, we are also positioned in heaven at the same time. We carry God's presence with us because the Holy Spirit is in us here on earth and we are in Christ, present with him in heaven.

How brilliant! We have solutions from heaven available for any problem we face.

This is what Jesus meant when he told us to pray for his will to be done on earth as it is in heaven. Our spiritual positioning in heaven means that we can receive from heaven. Our physical positioning on earth means we can release heaven's solutions on earth. I find this incredible and it gives me hope and courage every day.

During another time of sanctified imagination, Jesus led me down some stairs to a basement full of rooms with locked doors. Jesus explained that behind each door were blessings, giftings or opportunities waiting to be unlocked. Many doors were waiting for the right time for the Father to unlock them, but others were doors that had once been opened but which I had relocked – which meant I was missing out.

Later that evening, I was ministering to a person and I felt prompted to take them through the same exercise. The person found this incredibly helpful in answering questions they had been asking God. I had received from heaven to help a situation on earth.

Similarly, through experiences like this, I have received answers for my business, my family and my role as an elder in our church.

Understanding our positioning is key to understanding how powerful we are. So often we see ourselves as inadequate, unable to influence and change situations and environments around us. We can be like the ten spies who came back from the promised land with the perception of being like a grasshopper.

We are positioned for influence. We are positioned to encounter God and release what we receive from him on earth.

> On the last and greatest day of the festival, Jesus stood and said in a loud voice, 'Let anyone who is thirsty come to me and drink. Whoever believes in me, as Scripture

has said, rivers of living water will flow from within them.' (John 7:37–38)

We have established that we are designed and equipped to encounter God; in this chapter we have further established that we are also *positioned* to encounter God.

EXERCISE 5:
BRINGING THE WORD TO LIFE

> All Scripture is God-breathed and is useful for teaching, rebuking, correcting and training in righteousness, so that the servant of God may be thoroughly equipped for every good work. (2 Timothy 3:16–17)

Whenever God speaks to us, what he says will never contradict the Bible. The better our appreciation and understanding of Scripture, the more confident we can be about being led by the Spirit.

Jesus said to the Samaritan woman in John 4 that true worshippers will worship God in spirit and truth. To become mature Christians, we need both Scripture and the Spirit to lead and empower us.

> The Spirit gives life; the flesh counts for nothing. The words I have spoken to you are spirit and they are life. (John 6:63)

Receiving Scripture and hearing from the Spirit bring life.

In this exercise I want to encourage you to bring Scripture to life in your imagination. You could do this with any story in the Bible, but for this exercise, can I suggest you use the story of the Samaritan woman in John 4.

Read the story a couple of times to become familiar with it. Then relax and close your eyes and imagine yourself in the story.

The beauty of this sort of imaginative exercise is the ability to imagine yourself as *any* character in the story, or to remain a casual observer.

Imagine yourself as an observer. What do you notice? Can you imagine the emotion? Is there any humour in Jesus?

Now imagine yourself as the woman coming to the well. Jesus asks you for a drink. How do you respond? What does he want to reveal about your past? What truth does he speak to you?

His words are life.

ACTIVATE

> Follow the way of love and eagerly desire gifts of the Spirit, especially prophecy. For anyone who speaks in a tongue does not speak to people but to God. Indeed, no one understands them; they utter mysteries by the Spirit. But the one who prophesies speaks to people for their strengthening, encouragement and comfort.
> (1 Corinthians 14:1–3)

If we choose to go after God-encounters and desire them, God will activate us. Commit yourself to encountering God and it will happen!

One of the ways God will activate those who pursue him is in the area of encouraging others.

We continually need encouragement, but often find it lacking. Instead we are regularly exposed to negative attitudes and comments. It is common to hear criticism of what we do and who we appear to be, but much harder to find encouragement. I believe Christians should be the most encouraging people on the planet. This is why God gives us the gift of prophecy. Prophecy is for strengthening, encouraging and comforting. Paul says to especially desire the gift of prophecy because, when this gift is used, it calls people to be more than they are at present. It calls out their gold and turns people towards their potential. Strength, courage and comfort are in such short supply, yet we all need a regular injection of them. Frequent doses are required to increase our health and wholeness, to enable us to reach our potential. This is one of the reasons why it is so important to meet regularly with other Christians so we can strengthen, encourage and comfort each other.

As part of my journey, I determined to live a lifestyle of encouragement. I am getting better at it but still trip up occasionally! Not all encouragement is prophetic; however, all prophecy should be encouraging. I believe the more we live an encouraging lifestyle, the more we will prophesy, sometimes without even realising it. My experience has been that the more we encourage, the more we are activated.

Sanctified imagination has been a powerful tool in terms of increasing my ability to help people be built up in their spirit and have God-encounters. This happens through receiving an increase in prophetic words to share but also, while I am ministering to people, I encourage them to have their own imaginative experiences. I help them get started with an exercise so they encounter Jesus and hear him speak encouraging words to them directly.

During one of these times, I was in the throne room of God and walking with Jesus until we came to the Tree of Life. I asked Jesus if he could explain the leaves.

He pointed at some and said, 'You see the ones with an orangey hue' – at that point I noticed the leaves were all different colours – 'they can be used for your nation. Those leaves are designed for the healing of broken promises. Your country hurts because of the betrayal of broken promises.

Your government can't bring healing, despite their best efforts. Money won't bring healing, though it may be asked for. Only the church can bring healing for past broken promises through the leaves I have provided.'

This occurred when I was in bed, and I fell asleep once Jesus had spoken. When I woke the memory of this experience stayed with me quite strongly. I wondered, *What are the leaves and how are they applied?*

A few days later I was at a meeting and shared this story with a couple of friends. One of them was a young lady from our church who is a gifted leader. As I finished sharing the story, I started to prophesy over this young woman that she was an orange leaf and that God was raising her up to start initiatives and provide leadership that would be part of bringing healing to our nation of New Zealand.

I continued to share prophetic words with her, but now the previous conversation I had with Jesus meant even more. I now believe it is possible that the leaves on the Tree of Life symbolise God's people being activated to bring healing to nations. These are people who are connected to heaven, hear Jesus, and bring healing to nations from the divine impartations they receive. Through being positioned, these people are able to take the spiritual leaves from the Tree of Life and apply them to physical situations on earth. Uniquely gifted, they are called and positioned by God to touch the broken parts of society so that society is restored to what it should be.

Receiving this word from Jesus in my imagination and then allowing a prophetic outworking of that word is an example of sanctified imagination partnering with the prophetic in a way that brought strength, courage and comfort.

I received strength in my thinking, the person I prophesied over received encouragement and the people who will be ministered to when the prophetic word is fulfilled will receive comfort.

When we connect with God using our imagination, the experience will always strengthen, encourage and comfort us, but also increase our prophetic activation. As we learn to hear from heaven through our imagination, our ability to speak prophetic, encouraging words to others will grow. We will be able to minister to others directly from Jesus.

Jesus is a far better counsellor than I am. He can speak truth directly to our needs, bringing healing and freedom, without embarrassment. There are many ministries that make use of Jesus speaking truth directly to a person including Theophostic Counselling and Sozo. In the past, when I have been ministering to people, I have usually started by listening to a problem they want God to fix. They are looking to me, as the one ministering, to come up with the solution, either through godly advice or a miracle. This is a valid approach to ministry, and at times people have experienced breakthrough when I have ministered this way. But at other times I have felt people leave without receiving what they were looking for.

Unless God reveals the answer or provides the solution, all I can do is leave my fingerprints on people as I put my hands on them. Despite my greatest compassion for them and despite my best advice, I don't really know what people need to hear to solve their problems. Without revelation from God all I can do is guess. *Yet Jesus has the answer!* He knows exactly what we need to hear, and he is always speaking. All we need to do is listen.

Jesus always speaks a word that brings strength, courage and comfort. I am amazed how often people say Jesus spoke words that were very helpful, just what they needed to hear. God is so good!

The cue for me to use this tool in ministry is receiving revelation about an imaginative scene that the person will connect with. I was recently at another church with three pastors, each with a strong prophetic gifting. The four of us had been invited to minister to their leadership team.

One of the women from their leadership team had been receiving powerful prophetic words from the three pastors and I felt that, had I prophesied, I would have simply been repeating what had already been said. Instead of prophesying, I asked the lady to imagine she was in a dance hall, sitting on a chair at the edge of the room looking out over the hall. An orchestra was playing. Once she acknowledged she could see herself in the room, and could hear the music, I asked her to imagine Jesus walking over the floor to her, taking her by the hand and asking her for a dance. (I ask the person receiving ministry to acknowledge that they can see Jesus.) I then said, 'Go ahead and dance, and as you dance with Jesus feel free to talk with him.' She spent the next half hour or so being ministered to by Jesus and had a wonderful time.

I have encouraged people to imagine themselves tramping, hunting, having coffee, dancing, in a scenic place, going into a house of creativity – each room holding different creative resources for worshiping God, and so much more. I find it amazing how God shows me a connection point that is relevant to the person being ministered to. We are all unique.

Taking steps of faith and combining physical action with our imagination can activate us.

I normally lead our church's pre-service prayer time which starts at 9 a.m. I like to get there at 8.30 a.m. so I can spend some time soaking with Jesus. On a recent occasion I went into the throne room in my imagination and took a big drink from the Water of Life. I then went over to the Tree of Life and looked at the fruit. I observed the word 'joy' written on the fruit, so in my imagination I plucked one and started to eat.

I have found mixing a bit of physical action sometimes enhances what is going on in my imagination. When I drink from the river, I physically carry out the action of dipping a cup or a bucket into the water and lifting it up and drinking from it. When I eat the fruit from the tree, I act like I am eating fruit. Doing this helps activate faith around my imagination.

On this occasion after eating the fruit labelled joy, I took another step of faith and chose to laugh. From the Bethel Firestarters course which I facilitate at our church, I have learnt that we don't have to laugh to be joyful; but if we never laugh due to the joy of the Spirit, then perhaps we aren't as joyful as we think. If I have eaten the fruit of joy by faith and received joy, then why not laugh? While eating the fruit I didn't feel any Holy Spirit empowered laughter, I just felt normal. By faith I started laughing. Once I started to laugh, I became *drunk* in the Spirit, laughing freely, struggling to stand. I was like that for the next hour and a half. I haven't been drunk in the Spirit very often, but mixing sanctified imagination with faith can have powerful consequences.

Very occasionally there has been a blockage when I have

been ministering to people. Sometimes people can struggle with their imagination and the concept of seeing Jesus or hearing him speak. We will look more closely at these blockages in the next chapter.

For now, let us summarise what we know. We are designed. We are positioned. We are equipped. And we can be *activated* to encounter God and hear him speak. Wow!

Before we close this chapter, I would like to provide a guideline for your safety. If you ever have a negative experience with your imagination, ask Jesus for help. Condemnation, inappropriate thoughts, and words designed for controlling others do not come from heaven and can be rejected. Thoughts of fear, doubt, anger, condemnation and control are all inappropriate and Jesus will always help us overcome these types of thoughts when we ask. Some years ago I had fallen into a pattern of inappropriate thinking at night. Each night was the same. Finally, I came to my senses and cried out to Jesus for help. Immediately the power of the thought pattern was broken, and I haven't experienced it since.

The Bible says,

> And everyone who calls on the name of the Lord will be saved. (Acts 2:21)

Salvation is complete and includes our thought life. When we call on the Lord to redeem our thinking, he will save us and break the power of any thinking that damages us. The apostle Paul has this to say on the subject:

> Those who live according to the sinful nature have their

minds set on what that nature desires; but those who live in accordance with the Spirit have their minds set on what the Spirit desires. The mind controlled by the sinful nature is death, but the mind controlled by the Spirit is life and peace. The sinful mind is hostile to God; it does not submit to God's law, nor can it do so. Those controlled by the sinful nature cannot please God. You, however, are not controlled by the sinful nature but are in the Spirit, if indeed the Spirit of God lives in you. And if anyone does not have the Spirit of Christ, they do not belong to Christ. But if Christ is in you, then even though your body is subject to death because of sin, yet your spirit is alive because of righteousness. And if the Spirit of him who raised Jesus from the dead is living in you, he who raised Christ from the dead will also give life to your mortal bodies through his Spirit, who lives in you. (Romans 8:5–11, TNIV)

We have many promises in the Bible like this one which tell us that, if we are living by the Spirit, submitted to God, then we can have confidence that God will help us with our thought life. If you are struggling, like I was, with an aspect of inappropriate thinking, be encouraged – breakthrough is available.

Through the power of the Spirit our mind becomes a wellspring of life, not only enriching ourselves, but also becoming a blessing to others as the Spirit activates it.

EXERCISE 6:
Yes, Lord

I am the true vine, and my Father is the gardener. He cuts off every branch in me that bears no fruit, while every branch that does bear fruit he prunes so that it will be even more fruitful. You are already clean because of the word I have spoken to you. Remain in me, as I also will remain in you. No branch can bear fruit by itself; it must remain in the vine. Neither can you bear fruit unless you remain in me.

I am the vine; you are the branches. If you remain in me and I in you, you will bear much fruit; apart from me you can do nothing. If you do not remain in me, you are like a branch that is thrown away and withers; such branches are picked up, thrown into the fire and burned. If you remain in me and my words remain in you, ask whatever you wish, and it will be done for you. This is to my Father's glory, that you bear much fruit, showing yourselves to be my disciples. (John 15:1–8)

There is incredible power and intimacy in abiding in Jesus. Living out of our own strength as Christians is an oxymoron. To be a Christian is to live by the Spirit. Remaining in

Jesus implies having his presence, his communication and his authority active in our lives.

Letting Jesus take charge of our imagination, and partner with us, takes our sanctified imagination to a place of intimacy, revelation and power.

For this exercise we are going to allow Jesus to lead us. We are also going to combine parts of two previous exercises. Get comfortable and then imagine yourself in heaven walking down the streets paved with gold, mansions on each side. The street leads to the throne room. As you arrive, imagine a big door at the entrance. Engage in thanksgiving until you notice the door open. As you enter, ask Jesus where he is and then go to him. Ask Jesus what he wants to do and allow him to lead. You may want to write the experience down.

On one occasion when I did this, I imagined Jesus washing my feet. When Jesus had finished he asked me, 'Do you know why I washed your feet?' I asked him to tell me why, and felt Jesus respond, 'I, your Lord am happy to wash away the muck of each day that has dirtied your feet without any judgement. Therefore don't judge others for what they are going through. Allow your love to cover over many failings.'

Denise and I were going through a niggly phase; I had started focusing on things that annoyed me. After this experience with Jesus I determined to stop focusing on the negative and show appreciation for even the smallest thing. This was one of the best things that happened in our marriage in recent times. Denise also caught on and it has sparked a new level of fun with each other.

Exercise 6: Yes, Lord

As you let Jesus take charge of your imagination, the Spirit of Truth will bring revelation to you that will cause you to grow and mature.

PRACTISE

> But solid food is for the mature, who by constant use have trained themselves to distinguish good from evil. (Hebrews 5:14)

This verse identifies one of the main strategies for spiritual growth. I suspect many of us would like God to zap us, removing any work and effort required so that we might be suddenly transformed. This is not the way spiritual growth normally occurs. Spiritual growth is predominantly a process and practice.

The Bible says we are changed from glory to glory (2 Corinthians 3:18 KJV) which implies a step-by-step process. Romans 12:2 tells us to be transformed by the renewing of our mind which again implies a process. Transformation comes as we renew our minds.

Hebrews 5:14 tells us that an ability or skill will mature through constant use, or in other words, practice. The verse tells us that, as we practise, we will make mistakes, discovering what is good and what isn't, but it is all training.

Whatever we set our hearts and minds to practise we will become good at. Running was my sport for many years and for a long period of time I would run 100 miles per week. Over time, I became a reasonable runner. I did not have a natural ability like some, nor did I have base speed. However, through diligent training I got to the point of being quite good at the sport. Constant practice matured my running ability.

What we set our hearts and minds to and practise, we will strengthen and become mature in. A number of years ago I was at a church supporting John, my senior pastor, who was preaching. I mentioned to John before the service that I felt I had some prophetic words for people and, as a result, John asked me to share them before he preached. After the service, one of the people I had shared a word with came to see me and told me I got their word completely wrong. Practising and taking risks will mean we will make mistakes, but it will also mean we will get stronger and more mature.

More recently, I was preaching at a friend's church and, before I preached, I shared a word I felt God had given me for the church. As soon as I shared it, the pastor got up to say something. That can either be a good sign or a bad sign when you are speaking! On this occasion, it was good! The pastor said, 'The church needs to know that at the intercessors' meeting this week we felt God say the same thing to us as what has just been prophesied.' That was really encouraging for me. I had been nervous about bringing the prophetic word. There was a risk. I exercised faith. Practice brings maturity.

At the start of this book, I talked about believing the lie that I wasn't designed for God-encounters. But there came a point when I recognised this as a lie and determined to change my thinking. That change did not take place through being zapped by God. It came from being determined to go after God-encounters and hearing him speak. It came from my desire and grew through practice. It has been a process of development and practice for nearly ten years and it continues.

Our Baptist denomination has a three-day retreat in Hanmer each year, where pastors and leaders gather together to fast, worship and seek God. I have made a point of being there every year, actively looking for God-connections. As I went after these God-encounters, a shift started to take place in me, and it was through this shift that I discovered what I have described as sanctified imagination. It came out of diligently going after what I set my mind to. As I have practised imagination exercises for myself and assisted others, my maturity in using it has grown.

If you want to prophesy, set your mind to go after prophecy. Take risks and perhaps make some mistakes and you will grow in maturity through the process.

If you want to operate in the gift of healing, again, diligently go after it. Take risks and make mistakes and you will grow in maturity through the process. This has been happening at our church for a number of years now. As we have diligently gone after healings, the number of people being healed has increased. Many people don't experience immediate healing, but a number do. And this number increases the more we practise.

If you want to go after God-encounters, diligently go after them. Take risks and practise. Sanctified imagination is a great way of doing this.

What if you struggle with imagining things, as some people do?

First of all, realise you have an imagination. We all have an imagination. Some may be undeveloped, but the facility is there. There is an easy way to check if you have an imagination. Is there anything you are afraid of? If there is, where does the fear come from? The fear exists because you can imagine something going wrong. If you are unable to imagine it, why would you be afraid? Fear is a negative example of your imagination! Your imagination just needs training and maturing. This is one of the reasons I have included different exercises in this book; they will help you train and develop.

However, for some people, there does seem to be a barrier in seeing themselves in this place and experiencing God.

If this describes you, then one of the causes may be that what you expect in your imagination, and what you experience in reality are different. Perhaps you are expecting to see images which are crystal clear, but you don't. All you conceive is ideas and concepts, so you think you are not imagining anything. Some people *do* see clear pictures. Some people visualise in colour, others in black and white. I normally see what I imagine without clear pictures. My imagination is more about impression and sense. This does not make it any less real, or less helpful in hearing God.

Don't worry about what is not happening but be thankful for what *is* happening. Thankfulness is the key that opens the door for more, as we have discussed.

Perhaps you are struggling to imagine Jesus. You can picture yourself in familiar surroundings but do not see Jesus in your thoughts. He is there. One of the attributes

Practise

of God is that he is omnipresent; that means he is everywhere. Everywhere includes your imagination. Jesus is there even if you are not seeing him. It requires a step of faith to believe Jesus is there. By faith, act as though Jesus is there and talk to him. As you practise, you will increasingly sense his presence and discern him speaking to you.

Sometimes, if people do not hear Jesus speak through any of the many ways he communicates, there may be a barrier. Such a person may need help. This is just part of the process and development for them.

I have discovered that each step we take makes room for the next. My wife Denise and I discovered this principle as we had to work through aspects of her depression. Medication made room for counselling. One type of counselling made room for the next. Counselling made room for learning strategies. Strategies made room for ministry from God. Each step made room for the next.

This is the same with your imagination and encountering God. It is one of the reasons I have included different types of exercises in this book. Do not worry about what is not happening. Give thanks for what is happening! Allow God to grow what is happening and you will discover you are making room for the next step.

May you continue to grow in your encounters with Jesus and in hearing his voice. This is my prayer for you.

EXERCISE 7:
Keep It Simple

If you have been struggling with using your imagination (the thoughts, pictures, ideas that come into your mind), this exercise is for you. It will help you to train your imagination.

Start with imagining something small. Choose a flower, preferably one you are familiar with. Now imagine the flower in a vase on a table you are also familiar with. Now think of yourself sitting at the table; imagine a favourite drink in your hand.

You may not see the picture vividly, it may be more of an impression and that is fine.

Finally, imagine Jesus sitting across the table from you, having the same drink as you. Take a risk, ask him what he thinks of you. Wait for an answer. Grab the thoughts that come to your mind at that point and do not try to reason them away. Write them down. If they strengthen, encourage or comfort you, they are from Jesus. Be encouraged.

GROW

> Do your best to present yourself to God as one approved, a worker who does not need to be ashamed and who correctly handles the word of truth. (2 Timothy 2:15)

The beginning and end of our theology should always be Scripture. I learnt 2 Timothy 2:15 by heart as a young Christian, realising there is a strong connection between God trusting us to do his work, and our understanding and use of Scripture. For over 40 years, I have read and studied the Bible almost every day. I have found the simple exercise of regular reading to be incredibly helpful in decision-making and in life generally.

Sanctified imagination is a tool for strength, courage and comfort, as we have discussed in a previous chapter. It helps us grow in our identity, our love for God and our compassion for others. We are instructed to test everything and to hold on to what is good (1 Thessalonians 5:21). Scripture is our test, our base for what is good.

One of our senior pastors, Sandra Alpe, recently started a monthly creative worship service on a Sunday evening where many options for worshipping and connecting with God are available. At a recent service, I was imagining myself walking with Jesus along the streets in heaven. This was an occasion I had asked Jesus where he would like to meet and where he would like to go.

As we walked the streets, we came to a mansion and Jesus said to me, 'This is the place I am building for you.' We went inside and entered a large reception area that had paintings on the wall and a sweeping staircase to each side. Jesus said, 'People have no idea how many others have been touched and influenced through the ripple effects of what they did on earth. There is an eternity for people to discover everyone who had influence in their lives directly or indirectly and, naturally, people want to say thanks. You need a good reception area for welcoming people.'

We then moved into a side room which had really comfortable couches. We chatted for a while and Jesus encouraged me that he could be trusted with regards to my business.

When we left there, we went into the next room which was empty apart from a sketchbook on a table. Jesus told me this was my creative room. Heaven stretches for eternity; there is always room for something new. We are made in God's image and creativity is part of us. Opportunity to express this creativity exists in heaven.

Jesus then took me across the hall to a room full of trophies. He said, 'These are the trophies you earned every time you obeyed my promptings.' In the centre was a large ornate cabinet with the word *pointless* written across the bottom. I felt Jesus laugh as he said, 'These trophies hold a special place: they are for all the times you took an extra step of faith and it seemed to flop, or didn't make sense to you, but you did it anyway. Those times are of immense value.'

The mansion Jesus was building for me wasn't finished

but I felt it would be by the time I got there. At the back of the mansion, the ground was made up of rolling, low-lying hills, barren and empty. Jesus said, 'It is empty so you can make it the way you want it when you get here.' Then the imagination time finished as I spent time worshipping.

Later in the meeting I was prompted to minister to one of the men who had come, and take him into his imagination, getting him to picture what I had just experienced. When the meeting finished I caught up with him to ask how the experience had gone for him. He said, 'It was great. Jesus and I were ripping walls out and changing rooms around, making the mansion the way we wanted it. We were having a great time!' That was so awesome to hear. We are all unique! Jesus says he will make each of us a place in heaven. They won't be cookie-cutter designs.

What do I take from this? Firstly, there is no need to say this was a literal vision of heaven. I think our minds are too limited in this body, and heaven too real for us to be able to describe it literally. I think we translate what we see in heaven into things we are familiar with. With any of our imaginations, there is no need to take what we experience as literal.

We take what fits with Scripture and allow it to deepen our understanding. Take what brings strength, courage and comfort and happily throw away the rest.

In the mansion illustration, we know from Scripture that Jesus is preparing a place for us because he said he would. There is much for us to do in heaven and creating new things for heaven could easily be possible.

Nothing we do in Jesus' name is wasted. It has eternal value. Even the things we thought were a waste of time have value, which the apostle Paul confirms in his writings. Lastly, rearranging our mansion into the way we want it, in our imagination, reminds me that we are all unique. We don't have to be like anyone else and neither do our encounters. What Jesus prepares for me will be different to what he prepares for you. We are free to be the people he made us to be.

I find sanctified imagination to be incredibly revelatory and I hope you will as well. If you use these points as a safety net, you will have a great time exploring your imagination with Jesus.

Remember the illustration of the library. God is continually speaking. Listening to what he is saying to you is key to becoming everything you were designed to be. Revealing your identity. Discovering breakthroughs. Fulfilling your calling.

I pray that as you experiment with this tool you will prosper even as your soul prospers, that your mind will continue to be renewed with the mind of Christ, and that you will impact the world around you.

I would love to hear the stories of your experiences with the sanctified imagination. You can email me at:
encounterministries@sabc.org.nz

ABOUT THE AUTHOR

Robert Norriss is a husband and the father of three awesome grown children. He owns and manages an engineering business with his brother that has been operating since 1984. Robert has been an elder at Saint Albans Baptist Church for 20 years and is heavily involved in many aspects of church life. His passion is for people to come into a relationship with Jesus, reach their full potential in Christ and see God's kingdom grow around them.

www.ingramcontent.com/pod-product-compliance
Lightning Source LLC
Chambersburg PA
CBHW071412290426
44108CB00014B/1796